The Cotswo

The Cotswold Canals were originally conceived as two separate waterways.

The seven mile (12km) Stroudwater Navigation was opened in 1779 linking the River Severn to Stroud. In 1789, the twenty-nine mile (46km) Thames & Severn Canal was built to connect the Stroudwater Navigation to the River Thames at Inglesham, near Lechlade. This completed a through route from the River Severn to London.

In the 20th Century, following decline, abandonment and dereliction, the canals suffered some infilling and decay.

A society (now called the Cotswold Canals Trust) was formed in 1972 to protect and gently restore the two canals. A feasibility report highlighted the benefits of a restored waterway. As a result, in 2001, The Cotswold Canals Partnership was formed to speed the restoration of the two canals to their former splendour.

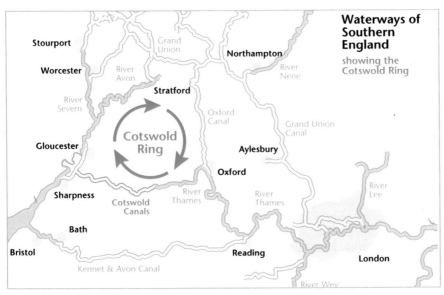

The 250 Year Story
- a short history of the Cotswold Canals

There were many early attempts to build a navigation from the River Severn to Stroud. In the 1740s Richard Owen Cambridge built a man-made waterway near Wheatenhurst for pleasure purposes. The Kemmett Canal was built between 1759 and 1763 from Framilode to the Stonehouse area. It featured the earliest known example of container traffic on an inland waterway.

The Stroudwater Navigation was built between 1775 and 1779 from Framilode, on the banks of the River Severn, to Wallbridge, Stroud. From the beginning, the canal was very profitable and a proposal was soon made for a link with the Thames and London. In 1781 a survey began of the line from Stroud to Cricklade on the River Thames which recommended the Stroud to Cirencester route. However, surveyor Robert Whitworth warned that trouble would be encountered on the summit which was to be built over "bad rocky ground". A Bill was introduced in 1783 and construction of the canal was expected to take six years. Josiah Clowes was appointed Resident Engineer. On 31st January 1785 the first vessel passed through the lock at Wallbridge in Stroud and went up the new canal as far as Chalford. The 241 feet rise from Wallbridge to the summit level at Daneway (near Sapperton) was completed in the summer of 1786 requiring 28 locks over a distance of seven miles.

At the summit came Sapperton Tunnel, the largest and longest canal tunnel built up to that time. Even to this day, its length has only been exceeded by two other canal tunnels in this country. It is 3,817 yards long and about 14 feet wide by 15 feet high. Work on the tunnel started in 1784 and after problems with the difficult ground and an incompetent contractor, was completed in 1789. The first boat passed through the tunnel on the seven mile summit pound to Cirencester in April 1789.

Work had proceeded meanwhile to the eastern side of the summit where the canal descends 129 feet over 13 miles via 15 locks to the Thames. The first boat reached the River Thames at Inglesham Lock on 20th November 1789. Lack of experience in the design and construction of canals resulted in a shortage of water almost from the first day. Numerous locks were built to varying lifts and due to the narrowness of the Golden Valley were constructed with intervening pounds of insufficient capacity. These problems, coupled with fissured limestone ground on the summit, made it wasteful of water. After using a wind pump for some years, the Company installed a Boulton & Watt single acting beam engine at Thames Head. In 1854 the Watt engine was replaced by a cornish beam engine of much higher capacity. The new engine could deliver three million gallons of water to the summit pound every 24 hours. The engine was scrapped in 1941 to aid the war effort.

Above: Wallbridge   Below: Brimscombe Port.
Both pictures were painted by unknown artists in the late 1700s.
Reprinted courtesy of Stroud District (Cowle) Museum.

The years 1820 to 1845 brought improvements to locks and constant maintenance kept leaks to a minimum. All locks between Chalford and South Cerney were shortened creating the characteristic double top gate recesses. Side ponds were added to some locks in the Golden Valley. The efficiency of the navigation was marked by steadily increasing receipts which peaked in 1841. However, competition from railways was growing and at the end of 1893 a notice was issued closing the canal east of Chalford until further notice. Despite protests, the canal remained closed, but eventually this led to the formation of a trust which took over the canal. The trust was formed by six other canal companies and five local authorities who reopened the canal throughout in March 1899. This achievement was short-lived as leakage on the summit caused the canal to close once again in June of that year.

In 1901 the canal was transferred to Gloucestershire County Council who began further restoration work. The length of canal from Cirencester to the River Thames was reopened in July 1902, from Stroud to Daneway in April 1903, and the summit pound in January 1904. The first vessel over the reopened summit was the *Staunch* in March 1904. The restored canal was still not completely reliable and was closed for at least twelve weeks of each year in 1905, 1906, and 1908 for repairs to the summit. It was also closed for twelve weeks in 1907 for repairs to Puck Mill Pound which was emptying in four hours through leaks in the clay puddle lining. The last loaded boat passed over the summit in May 1911 and only a few repairs were carried out in the next four years. In 1927 the canal was formally abandoned from Lechlade to Whitehall Bridge in the Golden Valley and in 1933 the remaining length to Stroud was also abandoned.

Entrance Basin at Framilode around 1900 (CT)

The Stroudwater Navigation, which had remained independent, carried on until 1941 when traffic of all kinds effectively ceased. It was abandoned by an Act of Parliament in 1954 despite vigorous lobbying to keep it open by local figures, notably Mrs Enid Airey. The fifteen years following the abandonment of the Stroudwater were the most destructive period in its history. Sections of the Thames & Severn Canal, abandoned in the early part of the century had also become derelict. Sapperton Tunnel suffered one roof fall and two side falls. Short sections of canal were returned to agricultural use at the eastern end. Brimscombe Port was filled in and became an industrial estate. Construction of the M5 motorway and its link road to the A38 resulted in the loss of Bristol Road and Meadow Mill Locks and the one mile of canal linking them. A flood relief scheme by Severn Trent Water Authority merged the canal with the River Frome for about 400 yards and resulted in the infilling of Whitminster Lock. A total of nine swing bridges were fixed.

Over the years, the remaining locks were allowed to decay with various service pipelines being installed at water level. British Rail enclosed the bridge over the canal at Stonehouse Court with an 'armco' tube and the road crossings at Stonehouse and Bath Road, Stroud were infilled. More recently, in 1987, the canal at Capel's Mill Viaduct was infilled to provide the Stroud East/West Bypass (Dr Newton's Way) although a bridge was incorporated into the scheme to allow for restoration.

The line of the canal is now protected in all District Council Local Plans. In 1996 Gloucestershire County Council commissioned British Waterways to make a corridor study which would supplement the engineering studies which had already proved the feasibility of restoration. The resulting report examined the cost benefit of full or partial restoration and concluded that in either case the benefits to the local community were extremely good both in terms of payback and number of jobs created.

Ownership of the majority of the Stroudwater remained with the original company. After abandonment, Gloucestershire County Council sold much of the Thames & Severn east of Chalford to the riparian landowners. The Cotswold Canals Trust maintained good relations with many of these, including particularly the Bathurst Estate which owns a large section of the canal including Sapperton Tunnel.

The Cotswold Canals Trust, which had started out as the Stroudwater Canal Society in 1972, promoted a reversal of the destructive processes and undertook specific restoration works using not only local volunteer labour, but also the visiting Waterways Recovery Group and other organisations. The result of all this effort has been that most of the canal corridor was declared a Conservation Area.

Today, The Cotswold Canals Partnership is co-ordinating the restoration of these two beautiful canals, its first major project being the 'Phase 1A' section from Stonehouse to Brimscombe. Keep up to date at www.cotswoldcanals.com

A Who's Who
of the Cotswold Canals

There's a group of organisations involved in getting the Cotswold Canals restored and sometimes there's confusion about who they are and what they do. Here's a very brief introduction with website details so you can find out more.

www.cotswoldcanalsproject.org

Formed in 2001 to drive restoration plans forward in phases along the whole 36 miles of the Cotswold Canals. Members include waterways groups, local councils, tourism and heritage bodies. The Phases of restoration can be seen on the maps in this book.

www.cotswoldcanals.com

With a current total over 7200, this is the membership organisation with roots in 1972. Many supporters join to follow the project in the Trust's quarterly magazine, *The Trow*. Their membership is vital as it shows funding bodies that there is public support for the project. Others promote restoration through its outlets at Saul and Wallbridge or visit local and national shows with the Trust's roadshow. Some members are involved in physical restoration and maintenance; although contractors tackle the big projects, there's still lots to do. Volunteer hours are measured and count as matched funding for Phase 1A restoration.

COMPANY OF PROPRIETORS of the STROUDWATER NAVIGATION

www.stroudwater.co.uk

They built, and still own, the Stroudwater Navigation (River Severn to Stroud). Now managed by volunteer directors, the major shareholder is a Trust which ensures that the Company is run for the benefit of local people. They have leased the canal to Stroud Valleys Canal Company for 999 years.

STROUD VALLEYS CANAL COMPANY

Follow the link from the menu at www.cotswoldcanalsproject.org

SVCC was set up in 2009 to acquire the property assets necessary to deliver restoration of the canal from Stonehouse to Brimscombe. Following restoration of the canal, the company will take on responsibility for operation, maintenance and repair. SVCC holds charitable status and is limited by guarantee.

www.stroud.gov.uk

After British Waterways withdrew, Stroud District Council became Phase 1A Lead Partner (Stonehouse to Brimscombe) for the Cotswold Canals Partnership using a funding package which includes money from the Heritage Lottery Fund, SW Regional Development Agency and others.

What to See

along the the Cotswold Canals

The following pages feature some of the main highlights of the Cotswold Canals. Whilst this is not a walking guide, it is quite simple to follow the towpath by consulting the map in the centre pages. Deviations to nearby roads and tracks will sometimes be required where the canal is in private ownership, mainly to the east. Care should be taken not to stray on to these sections. The Cotswold Canals are subject to restoration, so temporary towpath closures may be necessary where work is taking place. Descriptions are correct at the time of publication but may change due to restoration. For up to date news, visit the Cotswold Canals Trust's website www.cotswoldcanals.com

Credits

Thank you to the following contributors who have allowed us to use their material in this book. Without them, its publication would not have been possible. Each photo is marked with a number and initials with the key to the credits below - eg | 1 *DJ* |

AB - ANDY BERRY

CF - CLIVE FIELD

CT - COTSWOLD CANALS TRUST ARCHIVE

DJ - DAVID JOWETT

JF - (The Late) JACK FLEMONS - courtesy MICHAEL YOUNG

JG - JEFF GILLMAN - loan of photo

JM - JOHN MAXTED

KB - KEN BURGIN

MG - MIKE GALLAGHER see more   www.flickr.com/photos/76531763@N05/
                              photos at   www.mikegallagherphotography.co.uk

NB - NICK BIRD - see his website at www.cotswoldcanals.net

PC - PETER CHADWICK

PR - PAUL RUTTER

SD - STROUD DISTRICT COUNCIL

SE - SHIRLEY EASTO - loan of old postcards

TR - TOM ROUND-SMITH

      STROUD DISTRICT (COWLE) MUSEUM - photos of old paintings on page 5

      RICHARD FAIRHURST - cartographer of centre page map (updates - NICK BIRD)

Useful Maps

Ordnance Survey Landranger 1:50,000

162 Gloucester & Forest of Dean

163 Cheltenham & Cirencester

Ordnance Survey Explorer 1:25,000

168 Stroud, Tetbury & Malmesbury

169 Cirencester & Swindon

014 (covers very short section in west)

Framilode >

There are no current plans to restore the first section of the Stroudwater Navigation from Framilode to Saul - the Gloucester to Sharpness Canal provides a much better connection to the main waterways network.

1. The River Severn viewed from Framilode shows how difficult navigation must have been with sandbanks at low water and fierce tides racing up from the Bristol Channel. Trows were local vessels that used the river and the Stroudwater was built to accommodate their dimensions.

2. Framilode Lock is the first on the Stroudwater, seen here from the west bank of the River Severn. The lock is on private land and the first few yards of the canal are infilled. See the photo on page 6.

3. The Ship Inn, Framilode is one of the few remaining canal-side pubs. Local residents help keep some clear water amongst the reeds.

4. Saul Junction during a rare passage of a commercial vessel in 2005. This is an unusual waterways feature being a canal crossroads on the same level. Tall ships sometimes pass this way to events in Gloucester Docks, eight miles to the north.

10

5. A Trip Boat at Saul, operated by volunteers from the Cotswold Canals Trust, emerges from the Stroudwater past the navigation authority's Junction House. The Gloucester-Sharpness Ship Canal is 16 miles long, 16 feet deep and originally had 16 bridges. It was opened in 1825 well after the Stroudwater which was realigned to make the new crossroads.

6. Saul Marina is a recent addition to the junction area. Built in 2008, the marina boasts a capacity of almost 300 berths with an entrance off the Stroudwater.

7. Walk Bridge currently forms the first obstacle to navigation at the end of a quarter mile of canal which is home to the Saul Junction Boat Owners Club moorings.

8. Saul Junction from the air in 2006. The Gloucester to Sharpness Canal runs left to right whilst the Stroudwater forms the crossroads. The R W Davis & Son boatyard and drydock border the field which was to become the marina. The large red and green boats moored in 'The Pool' belong to the Willow Trust. The specially designed vessels are crewed by volunteers to provide people with disabilities the chance to get afloat. The Cotswold Canals Trust's Visitor Centre is just out of the picture on the right.

1. **Accommodation Bridge, Whitminster** which is around a mile from Saul Junction, was repaired in the 1990s by volunteers and contractors. The canal here is intact and in water but shallow and sometimes reeded. Close to this point is Fromebridge Mill on the A38 which is now a pub and restaurant.

2. **River Frome Bridge** is to the south of the original line of the canal which was filled in when the M5 was built in the early 1970s. This passage under the motorway will provide room for a separate channel for the canal on a slightly diverted line when restoration reaches this point.

3. **Westfield Bridge** is temporarily a 'bridge in a field' at the eastern extent of the missing mile of canal around the M5. Nevertheless, it has received attention over the years from volunteers and people working on schemes for the long term unemployed. The lock on this side of the bridge is infilled and is the first of five on the Eastington Flight. In the 1970s both were saved from demolition by a local farmer.

4. **Meadow Mill Spill Weir** near Eastington is a complex but fascinating structure restored by volunteers in the 1990s. It is located opposite an outfall of Oldbury Brook and allows the canal to be drained to three different levels. They may be less dramatic than locks, bridges and aqueducts but features like this are crucial for the control of water and the operation of a canal. Dock Lock, which is just about visible in the distance had been infilled in the 1970s but excavated and repaired by CCT volunteers in the 1990s. The towpath is unbroken from here to the other side of Sapperton Tunnel.

5. Pike Bridge has undergone many changes since it's first brick-built incarnation. This was replaced by an attractive Edwardian structure which in turn was demolished in the 1970s with large chunks dumped in nearby Dock Lock. The canal was infilled. In 2005, the Cotswold Canals Trust led a project to reconstruct the bridge you see today. The design mirrors that of the last bridge within the constraints of modern road safety standards.

5 NB

6. Pike Lock & Pike House follow immediately to the east of Pike Bridge. The lock had been infilled with a channel sloping down the middle to drain water away but was excavated and structurally restored in 1990. From this point the canal is technically navigable for almost a mile. A Cotswold Canals Trust trip boat operated here in previous years.

6 NB

7 & 8. Blunder Lock, Eastington was re-gated in 2013 (photo 8) after initial restoration by volunteers with new gates fitted in 1992. On 14th April that year the reopening ceremony was performed by Prince Charles.

It's not unusual for locks to have more than one name. This should be Lower Nassfield Lock but is better known as Blunder Lock, a name it acquired when the resident engineer reportedly built it on the wrong level in revenge whilst working out his notice after being fired.

7 DJ

The surrounding area was once the base for the Cotswold Canals Trust's plant and equipment compound but is now pleasantly landscaped making it a popular spot for a picnic.

8 AB

Eastington >

1. **Newtown Lock** was the first on either of the canals to be restored to full working order in 1991. This lifts boats to a gently curving length which passes below Newtown Roving Bridge. The bridge is so named because it carries the towpath from one side of the canal to the other.

2. **Bond's Mill Bridge** is the world's first 'plastic' lifting bridge. carrying a full Highways loading to service Bond's Mill Industrial Estate down the slope from the canal. The bridge is electrically operated and really *is* constructed of reinforced glass fibre! Whilst problems have been experienced with the road surface of the bridge, the glass fibre element has not caused any trouble.

The circular building alongside is a gun turret built during the Second World War. Its function was to protect the industrial estate which made a valuable contribution to the war effort. A plaque on the tower celebrates the new bridge.

3. **Ocean Rail Crossing** strides across and blocks the canal. The towpath passes beneath through an armco tube whilst the canal is relegated to a small six foot tube making this a major blockage. However there are high hopes that this will be rebuilt in 2015 when the railway line is due to be closed for work elsewhere.

4. **The Ocean** is a wide expanse of water to the east of the rail crossing. There is some debate about whether this predated the canal as a pond, perhaps associated with Stonehouse Court, a 17th century Manor House behind the church a little further along the canal which is now a hotel with a modern extension.

14

< Stonehouse

5 *MG*

Restoration of the canal from here to Brimscombe, over six miles further on, became known as the Phase 1A scheme. Phase 1B takes in the canal route from here back to Saul Junction.

5. Ocean Swing Bridge was a fixed low level structure until restored in 2012 as a fully operation swing bridge. A substantial commemorative bench alongside is one of many made by volunteers from reclaimed timber and raised funds for restoration.

6 *DJ*

6. St Cyr's Church can be seen from the Ocean standing alongside the most picturesque, and most photographed, section of the Stroudwater Navigation with the land sweeping away below the canal and up to the Cotswold Edge.

7. Nutshell Bridge is an unusual structure with two houses clustered around, Nutshell House on the east side being the most distinctive. They have no connection to the canal although they are linked by a passage under the bridge. There is no direct access on to the bridge from the towpath but there's another classic view through the arch back to St Cyr's Church.

7 *DJ*

8. Dredging at Stonehouse in 2011 photographed from a new road bridge that removed a blockage in 1999. Dredging is a necessary part of canal maintenance to prevent the bottom from getting too close to the top! The length of canal from the Ocean to Ryeford was dredged early in 2011 by the contractor *Land & Water*. Dredgings were of sufficient quality to be spread across a field further along the canal between Stonehouse and Ryeford.

8 *DJ*

15

1 MG

1. Upper Mills Bridge was built in 2010 as a fully navigable bridge to replace a fixed former swing-bridge at an entrance to Upper Mills industrial estate. There were some problems associated with its reinstatement as a swing bridge because of its proximity to a T Junction on the A419. Operation may have caused long vehicles to queue back on to the busy road so a solution was found by moving the canal slightly to the north to allow sufficient headroom. This was a good design solution to the challenge of a sloping entrance to the industrial estate.

2 SE

Wycliffe College, Stonehouse, Glos Bathing in the Lower Field.

2 & 3. Wycliffe College Boathouse was used by the nearby school as a base for rowing and other water-related pursuits until a better home was found right by the junction at Saul. The first photo is from an old postcard from around 100 years ago which contrasts with today's scene featuring the workboat *Wookey Hole,* owned by Stroud Valleys Canal Company and crewed by volunteers from the Cotswold Canals Trust.

3 MG

4 DJ

4. Skew Railway Bridge is an old railway bridge which crosses on unusual supports. This once carried the branch line from Stonehouse, through Dudbridge to a terminus at Nailsworth. Like many abandoned railway lines, it has a new use as a popular cycle track.

Within a few yards is another major road crossing. Haywards Bridge, built in 1993, did not remove (or create) a blockage as this was a new canal crossing to carry the Ebley Bypass. Proof that the restoration project was credible came with the building of this substantial crossing of the canal to full navigable dimensions.

16

< Ryeford

5. Ryeford Road Bridge used to carry a busy road to King's Stanley until the Ebley Bypass took away the traffic. It also featured some ugly redundant pipework which was removed in 2011 & 2012 to reveal its pleasing lines. Today, the *Cotswold Way* passes over the bridge.

5 DJ

Local residents have embraced the restored canal, keeping small boats alongside their properties. A new canal community perhaps?

6 MG

6. Ryeford Bridge viewed from the other, east side. The boat *Dragonfly* belongs to the Wilts & Berks Canal Trust and was a visitor in June 2012. It had been lowered into the canal on a temporary slipway back at Stonehouse so it could augment the CCT's trip boat operation at the *Stroud On Water* show, of which more later.

7 & 8. Ryeford Swing Bridge is a delightful pedestrian crossing of the canal which was restored by volunteers in the 1980s. It provides a private access for several canal-side cottages and takes only one member of a boat crew to operate from the non-towpath side of the canal.

7 MG

When a canal is restored, the line and associated structures must be maintained to keep them in working order. Though it's not quite the Forth Rail Bridge, the lattice work has received attention from today's volunteers with an ongoing requirement to keep the paintwork looking fresh.

8 DJ

To the east of the bridge, the towpath follows a narrow course between the dredged canal and the River Frome.

17

1 & 2. Ryeford Double Lock combines two standard locks into one by sharing the bottom gates of the top lock with the top gates of the bottom lock. The top lock chamber off-side wall collapsed in the 1980s when a burst water main in the nearby road above caused water to cascade down the hillside. The subsequent surge of water was responsible for dumping several feet of silt into Blunder Lock nearly two miles back along the canal. The Company of Proprietors of the Stroudwater Navigation used compensation funds to rebuild the affected sections of this massive structure. Full restoration followed in 2011 when the walls were fully repaired and gates fitted. There's no road access to the cottage by the lock.

The canal line above the lock used to be dry because of a long infilled section further along through Ebley. This allowed vehicle access to the local tip on the south side of the canal. Thankfully this is no longer in use and in 2007/8 the canal was excavated to Oil Mills Bridge.

3. Oil Mills Bridge was reinstated to remove a levelled road crossing. The original abutments were revealed as the blockage was excavated and a new concrete decking was installed on piling made within the old abutments.

4. Ebley was once know for the aforementioned infilled canal but this was excavated through a derelict industrial area in 2003. As part of planning consent, this was required of the developers who built the new 'Ebley Wharf' housing here. It's a popular place to visit to see (and feed) the wildfowl.

5. Ebley Mill is home to the offices of Stroud District Council but began life as a woollen mill. Being so tall, this is the most prominent building in the valley. Until 2003, the mill was surrounded by decaying industrial units but the land has been developed in stages to create an attractive new development.

5 *MG*

A new road bridge was constructed in 2007 as an alternative access to the old fixed low level bridge. A new pedestrian and cycle swing bridge access was constructed by the developers in 2013.

6 *MG*

6. Water at Ebley is controlled by a combination of devices. Several streams flow into the canal between here and Stroud so the resulting flow passes into the River Frome at Ebley via a spill weir. This towpath bridge crosses a larger spill weir which does the same job at times of high flows. Gates near the pedestrian entrance to Ebley Mill are installed for occasional use to prevent water causing flooding problems further down the canal.

7. Hilly Orchard Bridge is a recently constructed metal structure close to more recently built housing. Until 1992, the next quarter mile of towpath was closed to the public which meant taking a lengthy diversion to rejoin the canal at Dudbridge where another modern bridge was built to navigable dimensions.

7 *DJ*

8. Dudbridge during the successful *Stroud On Water* show in 2012. Stars of the show were boats from around the country. Their owners came to enjoy the canal and crowds came to see them just after a mile of canal was widened in a busy two week period.

8 *MG*

1. **Dudbridge Locks** can be found around a mile from Stroud centre. The high flow of water through here is caused by the streams that feed into the canal between here and Stroud. Before the canal was abandoned, they use to pass underneath the canal but were diverted into the canal which was narrowed from Stroud to Ebley back in the early 1960s. This heavy flow could have caused a problem but has been turned into an advantage.

2. **Dudbridge Hydro Scheme** was the way to take advantage of the 'problem' of high flows through this site. During 2012 and 2013, a large bypass system was constructed alongside the two Dudbridge Locks. This channels excess water around the locks and delivers it into a chamber which contains a turbine. The turbine house can be seen on the left in Photo 1. Accommodation has been made to enable fish to move from one level to another. The scheme has been part funded by donations but is expected to pay back substantial returns when electricity is sold into the grid and the proceeds used for maintenance of the canal.

3. **Chestnut Lane Swing Bridge** was built in 2012 to replace a fixed crossing. It's a substantial affair, too heavy for manual operation, so is electrically operated with hydraulics doing the work.

4. **A Slipway** was built close to Chestnut Lane Swing Bridge by volunteers around half a mile from Stroud centre during 2012. This was planned to enable boats to use the restored section back to Stonehouse after restoration of nearby Dudbridge Locks later in 2013.

5. The Site of Stroud Basin is close to the rear of the *Homebase* store at the end of the Stroudwater Navigation at Wallbridge. The Stroudwater had a terminus here, ending in a canal basin that is now infilled (seen here in 1961). It has been home to various businesses over the past years, some in modern units though some original buildings remain.

5 CT

6. Wallbridge Lower Lock is located a few yards from the start of the Thames & Severn Canal which branches off to the left of the old basin entrance. The slope above the lock has become steeper as the land above has been exploited for various business uses.

6 DJ

At the time of publication, planning permission had been granted for a development of residences for older people. This would stabilise the land and allow full restoration of the lock.

7. The Headquarters for the Company of Proprietors of the Stroudwater Navigation has a grand frontage which is not matched by the rest of the building. Indeed the window at the top right of the first floor is deceiving; there is no room behind, merely a space with the wall jutting out into thin air!

7 MG

When built, the facade would have looked down upon the terminus basin of the Stroudwater. Several businesses occupy the building today, including the Design Co-operative which was involved in the production of this book.

8. The Canal Enters Stroud around the bend from the headquarters where the new Stroud Brewery Bridge can be found.

8 DJ

1 CF

1. The A46 Road Crossing had been created in the 1960s by filling in the canal with a causeway after the canal was abandoned. There had been no bridge or crossing at this point until then. The photo shows the first stages of the work to build a new bridge with piling machinery in place.

2 DJ

2. Stroud Brewery Bridge was the result of a year's work by contractors. The general design of the bridge had been chosen from a number of options after a series of public consultations. During the work, traffic was diverted onto a network of roads that followed the original layout from the early 1960s. Stroud Brewery once bordered the canal here at Wallbridge, hence the name for the new bridge.

3 DJ

Wallbridge Middle Wharf lies below Wallbridge Upper Lock which was repaired in the 1990s by Stroud Valleys Project (with later help from the Cotswold Canals Trust) as a first step to revitalising this previously run-down area.

Since the bridge works were completed in July 2011, wild flower seed has been spread each spring alongside the canal creating a meadow effect close to the centre of Stroud.

4 MG

3. Modern Art? at Wallbridge with reflections, light and shade at Stroud Brewery Bridge.

4. HRH The Princess Royal declared the bridge and the lock beyond open on 10th February 2012. Princess Anne was still able to reach Stroud despite heavy snowfall the night before.

5 NB

5. Wallbridge Upper Lock in the mid 1980s. Until its demolition in 1990, the bridge used to span the head of the lock. This was an old entrance into the long-gone Midland Railway station yard, Stroud's second station. The competition, in the form of the Great Western Railway mainline station, still survives in town close to this point and features a fine example of a broad gauge railway goods shed.

6 DJ

6. Wallbridge Upper Lock was first restored in 1991 but the gates were ready for replacement late in 2011 when the walls also needed some minor rebuilding. The photograph shows Professor Mark Horton operating the paddle gear to empty the lock. He is a Vice President of the Cotswold Canals Trust and well known for his TV appearances in programmes with an archaeological theme in which he specialises and lectures.

7 DJ

7. The CCT Visitor Centre, Wallbridge is at the hub of a busy area for visitors at the gateway to Stroud Town Centre. A series of initiatives at Wallbridge included the creation of the Visitor Centre, the new cafe, the restored bridge, lock and canal. The 'Wallbridge Project' received two awards for the improvements made to this area.

8 NB

8. HRH The Princess Royal on the visit mentioned earlier. Here, she has boarded the CCT trip boat *Perseverance* which had been brought by road from Saul, its usual base. Passage through the lock took the party to Stroud Brewery Bridge below. A plaque by the lockside celebrates Princess Anne's visit. A good crowd celebrated too despite the freezing weather.

23

Stroud >

1. The Railway Viaduct in 1985, around a half mile from Wallbridge, featured the Thames & Severn Canal passing through one of the spans. The photo shows a volunteer work party keeping the channel clear.

2. The Railway Viaduct in 1987 seen from the east during work to infill the canal and replace it with the Stroud East-West bypass, now known as Dr Newton's Way. This was the last time the canal route was blocked which led to an outcry from the public. However, a bridge under the new road was built to allow for future restoration.

3. Capel's Mill Diversion in 2013 when a diversion around the blockage of around a quarter mile of canal was well underway. The photo is taken a few yards away from Photo 2 to the east of the viaduct.

< Bowbridge

4 MG

4. Capel's Mill Diversion in April 2013 seen from the west side of the viaduct. The canal here was already excavated and the earth was being stored in the channel whilst work proceeded on the other side of the viaduct.

5 & 6. Constructing the New Concrete Diversion Channel at Capel's Mill. When the new route was being designed, not only was the new road (built in 1987) to be avoided, but an old tip had to be skirted around, hence the piling to the left of Photos 3 & 6 which is holding back the ground above. With the water let in and the surrounding area landscaped, the new channel will soon blend into the scenery.

Photo 6 shows one of the Open Days in May 2013 when nearly two thousand people came to walk the new channel.

5 AB

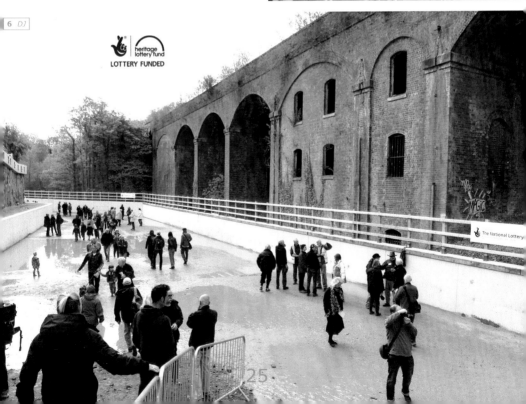

6 DJ

heritage lottery fund
LOTTERY FUNDED

The National Lottery

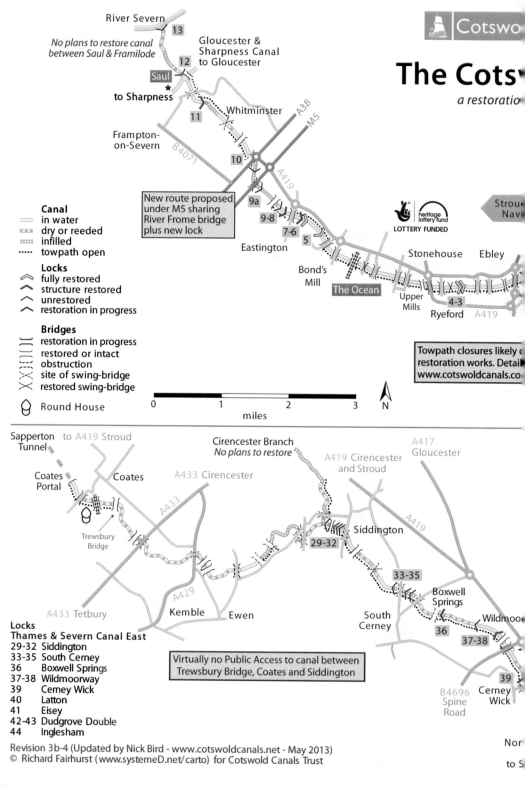

River Severn

No plans to restore canal between Saul & Framilode

13

12

Saul ★

to Sharpness

Gloucester & Sharpness Canal to Gloucester

11

Whitminster

Frampton-on-Severn

B4071

A38 / M5

10

9a

New route proposed under M5 sharing River Frome bridge plus new lock

9-8

7-6

5

Eastington

A419

Bond's Mill

The Ocean

Upper Mills

4-3

Ryeford   A419

Stonehouse   Ebley

Stroud Navi...

LOTTERY FUNDED / heritage lottery fund

Towpath closures likely ... restoration works. Detail... www.cotswoldcanals.co...

The Cots...

a restoratio...

Cotswo...

Canal
- in water
- dry or reeded
- infilled
- towpath open

Locks
- fully restored
- structure restored
- unrestored
- restoration in progress

Bridges
- restoration in progress
- restored or intact
- obstruction
- site of swing-bridge
- restored swing-bridge

Round House

0   1   2   3
miles
N

Sapperton Tunnel   to A419 Stroud

Coates Portal

Coates

A433 Cirencester

Cirencester Branch
No plans to restore

A419 Cirencester and Stroud

A417 Gloucester

Trewsbury Bridge

A433

Siddington

29-32

A419

33-35

Boxwell Springs

Wildmoo...

36

37-38

39

A433 Tetbury

A429

Kemble

Ewen

South Cerney

B4696 Spine Road

Cerney Wick

Locks
Thames & Severn Canal East
29-32   Siddington
33-35   South Cerney
36   Boxwell Springs
37-38   Wildmoorway
39   Cerney Wick
40   Latton
41   Eisey
42-43   Dudgrove Double
44   Inglesham

Virtually no Public Access to canal between Trewsbury Bridge, Coates and Siddington

Nor...

to S...

Revision 3b-4 (Updated by Nick Bird - www.cotswoldcanals.net - May 2013)
© Richard Fairhurst (www.systemeD.net/carto) for Cotswold Canals Trust

anals | Trust

ld Canals

alking map

Locks

Stroudwater Navigation		Thames & Severn Canal West	
1	Foundry	1	Wallbridge Lower
2	Dudbridge	2	Wallbridge Upper
3-4	Ryeford Double	3	Bowbridge
5	Newtown	4	Griffins Mill
6	Blunder	5	Ham Mill
7	Pike	6	Hope Mill
8	Dock	7	Goughs Orchard
9	Westfield	8	Bourne
9a	New M5 Lock	9	Beales
10	Bristol Road (Re-sited)	10	St Mary's
11	Whitminster	11	Ile's Mill
12	Junction	12	Ballinger's
13	Framilode	13	Chalford Chapel
		14	Bell
		15	Red Lion
		16	Valley
		17-18	Bakers Mill
		19-20	Puck Mill
		21-22	Whitehall
		23	Bathurst Meadow
		24-26	Sickeridge Wood
		27	Daneway Basin
		28	Daneway Upper

Thames & Severn Canal

Stroud

Wallbridge
2
Capel's Mill

heritage lottery fund
LOTTERY FUNDED

A46

3 Bowbridge

fins Mill 4
Thrupp

Ham Mill 5
Brimscombe

Chalford

19-21

Sapperton Tunnel
Daneway Portal

Hope Mill 6
9
10-13
14-16
22-28
Sapperton

oughs Orchard 7
17-18

8
Brimscombe Port
A419
Frampton Mansell
A419 Cirencester

ation Sections

3: Saul to The Ocean

A: The Ocean to Brimscombe Port
Brimscombe Port to Gateway Bridge
Gateway Bridge to Inglesham

wold Canals Trust Visitor Centres are at
& Wallbridge Lock, Stroud

Fairford A417
Cirencester

Burford A361

Lechlade

Dudgrove

42-43

44

Inglesham

Marston Meysey

Kempsford

Thames & River Thames
Severn Canal to Oxford

eway Bridge

Latton

Proposed new route and lock

41

Eisey

No Public Access to canal between
Ampney Brook, Eisey and Inglesham

40

Old course

Ampney Brook Aqueduct

A419 Cricklade, Swindon

Cotswold Canals Trust
Bell House, Wallbridge Lock, Stoud. GL5 3JS
www.cotswoldcanals.com

Bowbridge >

1 DJ

Late in 2012, it was announced that the next section of Phase 1A would be restored mainly by volunteer labour. This was because it was one of the easier lengths and would keep restoration progressing up the valley until money was released into the Phase 1A restoration from the sale of development land at Brimscombe Port.

2 MG

1. Bowbridge Lock & Bridge can be found around a mile out of Stroud. The bridge was culverted after the canal was abandoned. It was due to be fully restored during 2013. Following the building of a retaining wall above the lock, a volunteer scheme was due to start to restore the lock.

2. Towpath Works at Bowbridge are part of the towpath upgrade for the whole of the Phase 1A length of canal. This party is organised by the Cotswold Canals Partnership but other groups are led by REACH, an organisation which co-ordinates people undertaking Community Service.

3 DJ

3. Stanton's Bridge was the first structure to be restored by volunteers in the early 1970s. Such was the dry state of this stretch of canal that it was let out for grazing before volunteers excavated by dragline and refilled the canal. Although the restoration society was then known as the Stroudwater Canal Society, for political reasons its first project was actually here on the Thames & Severn Canal.

4 MG

4. Griffin's Mill Lock was adopted by Cotswold Canals Trust volunteers as a longer term restoration project and was due to be completed late in 2013.

5. Jubilee Bridge has required volunteer work over the years including rebuilding of the towpath-side wall in the mid 2000s. It is believed that this elegant lattice-work bridge was built and acquired its name during one of Queen Victoria's Jubilee years. It carries one of the numerous paths that climb up the hillside towards Rodborough Common.

5 *MG*

6 *MG*

6. Ham Mill Lock was adopted by visiting volunteers from the Waterways Recovery Group. The photo shows the lock after the first work party. The coping stones have been pulled back so that the lock wall can be repaired. As this is a worksite, the lock has been fenced off.

Part of a western side bridge abutment collapsed back in 1989 when ivy was being cleared showing the power of vegetation to loosen brickwork. Thankfully no-one was hurt. Gloucestershire County Council had the damaged section of bridge rebuilt with a concrete repair finished off with a layer of bricks.

7. Above Ham Mill Lock, the stretch of canal is clear and popular with fishermen. There are fine views across the railway up to Butterow and Rodborough Common beyond. Equally, this part of the canal is easily seen from up on the hillside.

7 *DJ*

8 *DJ*

8. The Railway Line from Stroud to London runs alongside the canal. Here, 'steam special' *Bittern* heads towards Stroud though as it is heading downhill there's little steam or smoke to be seen. Along the canal is Bagpath Bridge. This view was taken from the same spot as Photo 7, although in November rather than summer.

1. **Bagpath Bridge** carries one of the many paths that come down the hillside to join the canal or cross to the valley bottom. They were used by workers who came down into the valley to work in the mills. Bagpath Bridge was subject to substantial restoration in the 1970s and maintenance work thirty years later.

2. **Abdela & Mitchell** was a steel boatbuilding business based at Hope Mill. Boats were often exported to places such as South America. Larger boats were built in sections and floated down to the Gloucester - Sharpness Canal. Isaac Abdela had taken over the boatyard when Edwin Clarke died in is thirties. After running into financial difficulties, Mr Abdela invented a Mr Mitchell who he claimed had invested money in the business. This seemed to satisfy his genuine investors and trading continued until 1921. The photo shows the first Clarke boat *Gordon*. The boat that stars in the film *African Queen* was reputedly built here.

3. **Factory Buildings at Hope Mill** squeeze out the canal route leaving only the towpath for around fifty yards. Plans are in hand to overcome this short blockage. The towpath remains in situ and the canal will run to the right.

4. **Gough's Orchard Lock** was restored by volunteers as part of the Phase 1A restoration scheme, undertaken mainly by visiting restoration groups such as the Waterway Recovery Group (WRG). The canal above here was infilled for around fifty yards in the 1960s as far as the *Ship Inn* at Brimscombe. This will be excavated to accommodate the canal.

< Brimscombe Port

Brimscombe Port was built as a massive trans-shipment depot. Locks from the River Severn to this point were built to accommodate trows - flat bottomed sailing vessels. The remainder of the route to the Thames provided for narrower, but longer, boats from that river, hence the need to provide for transfer of cargoes. The port also featured an island site which provided safe storage for goods including coal. A boat weighing machine was used to gauge loads and thereby ensure that the correct tolls were charged.

5. Thames & Severn Headquarters was a large three storey building accommodating clerks for the Thames & Severn Canal Company as well as warehouse space. Gloucestershire County Council acquired the canal in the early 1900s and took the opportunity to convert this building into Brimscombe Polytechnic. It remained as a school until the 1960s when it was demolished.

6. Historic View Across The Port
7. Hillside View from the South
8. The view from Port Mill Today

Although the original line of the canal through the port is now used for car parking, the land has been purchased and the long term plan is to develop the site with the restored canal at its heart. The sale to developers will release funds into the restoration scheme. In the meantime, some of the industrial units are let out to provide an income.

The eastern boundary of Brimscombe Port marks the eastern extent of the Phase 1A restoration length of canal.

5 CT

6 SE

Brimscombe, Basin.

7 CT

8 MG

31

Brimscombe >

1 DJ

2 DJ

3 JG

4 DJ

1. Brimscombe Port Walls were built to protect the boundary of the old port. The masonry has been restored using funds from the Heritage Lottery Fund (People's Millions) which was voted through by viewers of local TV.

Outside the wall were the old Bourne Mill buildings which were rescued from dereliction by a local businessman. He restored them and brought his *Noah's Ark* cycle business here from a premises it had outgrown in Chalford.

2. Bourne Lock is a dimensional one-off, built 90 feet long and just over 16 feet wide. This was done to allow the wider trows to reach the canal company's boatyard. From this point the locks were built 90 feet by around 12' 9" to suit boats from the Thames. A substantial obstacle to navigation above the lock is encountered where the railway crosses. All locks from Valley Lock, over the summit, to Wildmoorway Lower Lock were shortened soon after the canal was opened to save water. They were shortened by building new top gate recesses over an arched extension to the top cill (the actual step in the lock which is usually just below the top lock gates). These features are unique to the Thames & Severn Canal.

3. Brimscombe Station in the early 1960s. The station had sheds for the 'bankers', the engines that would help pull some trains up the steep gradient to Sapperton Railway Tunnel. The engine here is a Collett Class 1P 0-4-2T.

4. Beale Lock taken from almost the same spot as Photo 3 fifty years later.

< Chalford

5. St Mary's, Lock Chalford takes its name from nearby St Mary's Mill seen in the background. It is worth diverting for a few minutes up the steep steps on the eastern side of the substantial bridge to the railway crossing at the former St Mary's Halt which towers above the lock. Because the crossing is listed, it cannot be automated so is still manned. The embankment blocking navigation at the head of the lock was once spanned by a massive wooden viaduct designed in 1845 by the great Victorian Engineer Isambard Kingdom Brunel as part of the Cheltenham and Great Western Union Railway.

6. Ballinger's Lock from an old postcard is now buried below several garages. Chalford Round house is around the bend.

7. Chalford Round House from an old postcard seen across Sevilles Mill millpond. Chalford's Christ Church can be seen across what is now the A419.

8. Chalford Round House is the western-most of these five unusual buildings. This one and Cerney Wick Round House were built with more conventional conical roofs whereas three were topped off by a funnel shaped roof. This alternative arrangement featured on round houses which were in more remote locations and the strange design provided a cunning way of catching rainwater to channel down to underground tanks. Conventional hand-pumps were then used to draw the water.

After a spell in the 1970s as a small canal museum, Chalford Round House became a well-maintained private residence.

5 DJ

6 SE   Stroud Valley. Chalford.

Chalford Church, near Strou

7 SE

8 DJ

1 *DJ*

1. Clowes Bridge in the Golden Valley was named after a canal engineer. It is towards the start of one of the most popular lengths of towpath as it meanders through the Golden Valley. All through the year, but especially on autumn Sundays, walkers make their way up the beautiful valley to the pub at the top of the many locks. The scenery changes as the valley sides close in with houses clinging to the sides of the steep hills.

2 *DJ*

2. Puck Mill is the area at the heart of the Golden Valley where a quarter mile section of canal is owned by the Cotswold Canals Trust. This photo gives some idea of the climb required to reach the summit.

3. A Golden Valley Towpath View illustrates the beauty of the surrounding countryside that can be seen from the canal towpath.

4. Whitehall Bridge is notable for being the point to which the Thames & Severn Canal was abandoned from Lechlade in 1927. The canal was abandoned to Stroud in 1933.

3 *DJ*

The bridge is towards the bottom of the sequence of locks that climb to the tunnel. Below are Puck Mill Locks and above are Whitehall Locks, Bathurst's Meadow Lock, Siccaridge Wood Locks and finally the summit at Daneway Locks.

4 *DJ*

Some of the locks through Siccaridge Wood feature side ponds which curve away from the top of each lock and around the sides. This arrangement allowed for the storage of more water between the locks that were especially closely spaced.

5. Daneway Basin is to the far right of this old postcard view. It may be difficult to see through foliage, but is found between the top two Daneway Locks on the western climb to the summit. This formed a temporary terminus during the construction period of the canal and more especially Sapperton Tunnel. A better view can be had from the road which crosses the canal. The bridge here was under threat in the 1970s but was quickly listed and saved.

5 SE

6 DJ

6. The Daneway Inn, previously known as the *Bricklayers Arms*, was built around the same time as the canal and initially occupied by the navvies of the day who worked on the canal and especially the nearby tunnel. The pub car park is sited on the infilled top lock, which marks the start of the summit pound at 310 feet above sea level. The photo was taken from the bridge to the left of Photo 5.

7. The Tunnel Keeper's Cottage by Daneway Portal was occupied until the 1960s and the building remained intact until the 1980s. The overgrown piles of rubble which are encountered alongside the towpath about twenty yards from the portal today are the remains of the cottage. Theft and vandalism led to its unfortunate demise.

7 SE

CANAL TUNNEL, SAPPERTON

8. Daneway Portal in 2003. The portal had suffered from decay and vandalism but was restored in 1996 by a local stonemason. A path runs up to the right and along the back of the portal before climbing to the pretty Cotswold village of Sapperton from where the tunnel gets its name. Railway enthusiasts will be aware of the railway tunnel of the same name.

8 DJ

1. **Daneway Portal** in March 2013 with CCT Chairman Mike Guest (left) and CCT Vice-President Professor Mark Horton.

2. **Repair Work in 1982**

3. **Inside The Tunnel** on an expedition in 2008 through a brick-lined section

4. **Inside the Tunnel** showing a section through solid rock which is almost unchanged since the day it was built.

The building of Sapperton Tunnel on the Thames & Severn Canal was the greatest single achievement in the construction of the Cotswold Canals. At 3,817 yards long (over two miles), it was the longest canal tunnel in the country when built. Today it is still the third longest ever built in this country.

The builders dug shafts down from the surface which was 200 feet above in places. When the proposed line was reached they proceeded to bore their way from the bottom of one shaft to the next until the 'primary headway' was completed. This was opened out and lined with brick or left as bare rock. Even today the rock clearly bears the marks of their tools and drill holes where lumps were blasted away.

The effect on the landscape above the tunnel was the creation of small mounds of spoil. Today, the clumps of beech trees on top of these small mounds, at intervals across the countryside, mark the location of the construction shafts to the canal tunnel below. The shafts are capped by rotting timber and earth covers. They are very dangerous so *THESE MOUNDS SHOULD NOT BE INVESTIGATED.*

King George III was suitably impressed when he came to see the tunnel being built in 1788 during a stay in nearby Cheltenham. The stretch of canal outside the tunnel at Coates accordingly became known as 'King's Reach'. The tunnel took five years to complete and on its opening in 1789 boats were able to navigate inland between the Rivers Severn and Thames for the first time.

Trade on the canal declined in the mid nineteenth century and the last recorded passage of the tunnel was made in 1911 after which the cross country waterway link was progressively abandoned between 1927 and 1954. Falls occurred at the western end of the tunnel where it passed through Fuller's Earth.

5. Coates Portal Before Restoration

6. Under Restoration

7. In 1977

8. Coates Portal in 2003

The portals crumbled into the canal but the Canal Trust financed restoration of the eastern Coates Portal. The grand reopening was performed by Lord Bathurst in 1977 and nineteen years later, his son, Lord Apsley, was kind enough to do the same at the newly restored western castellated Daneway Portal. This isolated structure had suffered from vandalism over the years and the stonemasons were able to retrieve most of the masonry from the canal bed.

5 *JF*

6 *JF*

7 *JF*

8 *DJ*

Coates >

1. **Tunnel House Inn,** close to the eastern portal of Sapperton Tunnel, was once a three storey building until a fire gutted the structure in 1952. The pub was rebuilt some years later, one storey short. This photo shows the pub around 40 years before the fire.

2. **Tarlton Road Bridge,** photographed here in 1986, is a high road crossing and, once through, the towpath climbs so that it is high above the canal and level with the road.

3. **Coates Round House** is a few hundred yards from Tarlton Road Bridge. It was last inhabited in the 1950s. Although in private ownership, the round house was rescued from dereliction by the Cotswold Canals Trust but only after it had lost its inverted 'funnel' roof. Volunteers keep the old garden clear too. The canal is narrowed at this point which enabled the previous section to be isolated by inserting lengths of wood known as stop planks.

Just a few hundred yards east from here, at Trewsbury Bridge, the towpath ceases to be a Right of Way as far as Siddington, Cirencester.

4. **The Source of the Thames** is encountered when following a path from the canal towpath to the Thames Path. The location is marked by a stone which replaced a statue of Father Thames. This was moved alongside St John's Lock at Lechlade to protect it from vandalism.

The Thames & Severn Canal runs close by on private land up the slope from here. Is this the true Source of the Thames?

38

5. Thames Head Bridge survives but was superseded in the early 1960s by a new road alongside which passes over a culvert. A plaque on the face of the bridge records the canal's presence. Adjacent to the bridge, a wharfinger's cottage remains and is now a private dwelling alongside the old wharf.

5 KB

6. Smerril Aqueduct, seen here in the early 1900s, was removed shortly after abandonment.

6 CT

7. Smerril Aqueduct's Remains can be made out from the A429 to the north of Kemble. Whilst the original bridge under the aqueduct had been removed around 1930, the road was not realigned until the 1960s on a higher level. The photo from that time shows the fresh face of the cutting that reveals the profile of the canal embankment which led to the aqueduct.

Between the aqueduct and Halfway Bridge, the Cirencester Branch Line, from Kemble on the Mainline, once crossed the canal on a handsome stone bridge. It is understood that the bridge is intact under the underfill although the parapets have been demolished.

7 TR

8. Halfway Bridge, Kemble is so named as it is halfway along the Thames & Severn Canal between Stroud and Lechlade. It was restored in the late 1990s to preserve another brick built rarity on the Thames & Severn.

8 NB

After the canal was abandoned many humpback bridges were demolished as part of a 'job creation' scheme during the Depression of the early 1930s.

Siddington >

The towpath from Siddington is now a Public Right of Way as far as Latton near Cricklade.

1. Siddington Locks lie just below a junction (on private land). This was an arm to Cirencester for which there are no restoration plans at present.

The towpath lies alongside the first locks on the long, gentle descent towards the River Thames. This area was subject to extensive landscaping works by volunteers in the mid 1990s and is still immaculately maintained. The last of four locks has been replaced by a house, the only one on the whole 36 mile route.

2. Cowground Bridge is one more of the few remaining humpback bridges on the eastern half of the Cotswold Canals, one that wasn't destroyed as part of the job creation scheme during the Depression. Nearby lie ancient water meadows of the River Churn. The bridge was restored in 2012 by a group of local volunteers.

3. South Cerney Top Lock is at one end of Claymeadow Cutting. In the 1990s the towpath had all but disappeared but a mix of locals and visiting volunteer groups created a new level path. This emerges at the top lock of the South Cerney flight. The lock is infilled and cultivated by the owner of this and the old lock-keeper's house.

4. South Cerney Locks are buried in this field. During dry summer months the outline of the circular pounds and the chamber walls of the two lower locks in the flight can still be seen.

5. Boxwell Springs Lock was structurally restored by the Waterway Recovery Group in the mid 1990s. The stop planks which impound the water above the lock will be replaced by lock gates when the canal is ready for full navigation. Away to the right are the first signs of the Cotswold Water Park lakes which border the canal for several miles. They were formed after gravel extraction.

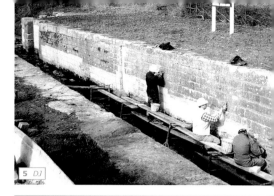

5 DJ

6 DJ

6. Wildmoorway Lower Lock is unique in having a side pond designed to save water during the operation of the lock. The side pond can be seen next to the towpath as it passes the lock chamber. The house which stands right on the lock-side was rebuilt in recent years after the original structure became derelict to the stage of having only one wall standing. The lock has been structurally restored (together with the bridge here) and the canal between the lock and the Spine Road was fully dredged as part of a major canal restoration event known as Dig '95. Six hundred volunteers spent a weekend working on locks, clearing towpaths and generally improving the canal-side environment.

7 DJ

7 & 8 Spine Road Bridge was built in 2004. Until then, the towpath was blocked by Spine Road which was built to allow removal of gravel thereby creating the Water Park. Funding was unexpectedly obtained to remove this blockage by building a new navigable bridge and safer route for walkers.

Decorative stainless steel features along the parapets portray reeds and bulrushes on this important gateway to the Cotswold Water Park.

8 DJ

1 JM

1. Dredging by Spine Road in 2010 close to the Water Park 'Gateway' Centre. New development is in evidence around this area and the nearest lakes in the Water Park are surrounded by houses and a hotel. Almost a mile or so of canal was dredged by volunteers (thanks to funding from the landowners, the Co-op) and re-profiled by contractors Gardiners (providing their machinery and operators at no cost).

2 KB

2. Dredging Towards Cerney Wick on the same project in 2010. The dredger was acquired by the Canal Trust in the 1970s and has been refurbished by skilled volunteers several times since then. It was first put to work in the 1980s at Ryeford near Stroud. The dredger has a set of wheels which allow it to be moved for short distances and has been transported by low loader.

3 NB

3. Cerney Wick Roundhouse and Lock are close to the village of the same name. The lock was restored by volunteers from the Cotswold Canals Trust in the early 1980s. The initial pointing job became a major rebuild when they realised just how poor its condition was. Makeshift top gates were installed in 1990 for cosmetic effect after being adapted from a redundant pair from the River Thames. There are reports that a bomb was dropped above the lock during World War II. Whilst it may explain a dip in the towpath, it appears that the round house suffered little damage whilst the pub along the road lost part of its roof!

4 CT

4. Cerney Wick Bridge was demolished long ago and replaced by non-navigable low level structure.

5. Latton Junction is with the North Wilts Canal, also subject to restoration plans, as is the Wilts & Berks Canal which it joins at Swindon. It is likely that a restored North Wilts Canal would join at a different location but this has not deterred volunteers from the Wilts & Berks Canal Trust and the Cotswold Canals Trust from working at Latton Junction which is usually in water. The North Wilts left to the south-east under a bridge and crossed the nearby leat by means of a small aqueduct into Latton Basin. The house here is now a private residence, but a public footpath passes behind the house where the North Wilts Canal's towpath can be followed.

5 DJ

6 CT

6. Weymoor Bridge is at one end of the short excavated canal at Latton Junction and is subject to plans for rebuilding as a traditional arched structure

7. Cricklade Wharf House provided accommodation for the wharfinger at its centre with wrap-around warehousing space. Similar buildings existed at Cirencester (demolished in 1975) and Kempsford (which survive). The canal is infilled here so the building sits between the busy A419 dual carriageway and a sliproad from Cricklade.

7 DJ

8. Latton Bridge was built in 1997 under the new A419 dual carriageway. The road could have created a serious blockage. but, after protracted protesting, lobbying and with funding from Gloucestershire County Council, a navigable culvert was incorporated under the road. Today, it is very difficult to see but is full of gravel and waiting for restoration of this section when it will be brought into use.

8 CT

43

1 MG

1. Eisey Lock is on private land close to the Cotswold Canals Trust's Eastern Depot. Nevertheless, restoration of the structure was complete by 2012. Once again this was achieved mainly by visiting parties from The Waterway Recovery Group. Although isolated at present, it was considered a worthwhile project to prevent further deterioration. All that's needed are gates when restoration proceeds in this area.

A variety of volunteer groups cleared the towpath and canal bed in this area.

2 MG

2. Rucks Bridge lies a hundred yards or so from Eisey Lock and was repaired by the same volunteers that restored the lock. They spent much of their time working on brickwork on and below the waterline. All is restored except the parapets which were presumed to have been removed to allow wide farm machinery to cross.

3 PC

3. Marston Meysey Round House in 1986 before its incorporation into a modern brick house. Being in a remote location it features an inverted 'funnel' roof to collect rainwater.

4 NB

4. Oatlands Bridge, Kempsford appears to be in the middle of a field down a short track. The bridge is in excellent condition although the canal, which was on a slight embankment, has been totally ploughed out of existence. There is a brick built into one of the parapets which has the words 'Stonehouse Brick Company' cast into it. The bricks for this bridge and probably other buildings in the area were brought by boat all the way from Stonehouse.

5. Inglesham Round House & Lock stand alongside the Thames where the Thames & Severn Canal joins this Royal river. Almost three miles of the canal cross private farmland until the last quarter mile which is owned by the Cotswold Canals Trust. The round house was bought by British Waterways when they were lead partner of the Cotswold Canals Partnership. After withdrawing from the partnership, the roundhouse was sold but the lock was gifted to the Trust for restoration.

6. Inglesham Round House seen on an old postcard with a view from the Thames.

7. The River Thames reaches the furthest point upstream where it is practical to turn a large boat. This is the confluence with the River Coln. The photo was taken from a footbridge over the river, a good viewpoint for the end of the Thames & Severn Canal which also emerges onto the river at this point. The river launch trip boat *Inglesham* belongs to the Cotswold Canals Trust.

8. Halfpenny Bridge in Lechlade is almost a mile from the end of the Thames & Severn Canal. In the summer, there's a good chance that you will see trip boat *Inglesham*. Cotswold Canals Trust volunteers offer trips and charters to the public from the Riverside Park in Lechlade.

The Thames weaves its way downstream across beautiful countryside and through towns and cities such as Oxford before turning tidal in London and ultimately flowing into the North Sea.

Paul Rutter is Biodiversity Director for the Cotswold Canals Trust. Here, he describes how a richer biodiversity can be achieved with canal restoration.

In Britain although we do not have the number and diversity of species found in your average rain forest, we can and need to improve our own biodiversity.

Sadly we have seen a continuing serious loss of biodiversity across the country. Fewer plants, insects and birds all caused by our insatiable quest for food production, transport and buildings, all impoverishing and fragmenting our landscape.

This dramatic change across the countryside has reduced the availability of a vital element that all plants and animals depend on, which is their own special niche. (nicher means to nest in French). A niche enables all animal and plant species to have a unique place in the eco-system while also satisfying needs such as shelter, food and reproduction.

1. **Fritiliary Butterfly** photographed in a wild flower meadow.

2. **A good example of a natural water edge along the canal** - something that's important to retain after dredging,

3. **Canal running along an old hay meadow** with bankside willow tree.

4. **A Wild flower meadow**

nd Biodiversity

A simple hole in a tree or wall, some rotting dead wood or long grass can all serve as valuable niches to numerous types of insect and animals.

The canal project offers a rare opportunity to enhance and increase niches for plants and wildlife along a green corridor of 36 miles, stretching from the Severn to the Thames.

While some more common wildlife and plants already have their niche, the restoration can increase the range and diversity of plants and wildlife that have been declining by taking a sensitive and measured approach in the restoration of the canal corridor.

By linking niches and habitat together along the canal corridor to the wider landscape will make it an even richer and more attractive place for people as well as for our wildlife.

The photos give just a few examples by way of illustration.

5 _MG_

6 _PR_

7 _PR_

8 _PR_

1. A Kingfisher canal-side at Bowbridge - as are many other varieties of birds.

6. Mixed age woodland fringe on water edge

7. Deadwood, standing and fallen, providing a niche to specialist insects as well as woodpecker.

8. Rare beetle on an ox eye daisy

47

1 DJ

Throughout this book there have been many examples of the achievements of the Cotswold Canals Trust. These would not have been possible without a vibrant membership which is still climbing and stood at 7250 in June 2013.

2 MG

Since 1972, volunteers have preserved, rescued and restored the fabric of the canals and watched whilst the public gradually recognised the value of their work. Volunteers cleared and maintained towpaths and generally improved the condition of the canals working with tiny budgets. There were numerous projects but three especially of note during the late 1970s and early 1980s were at Ryeford, Eastington and Cerney Wick.

Since 2001, the Trust has been a member of the Cotswold Canals Partnership which has secured major funding for larger projects undertaken by contractors. However, there's a greater need than ever for volunteers. Often, preliminary work is carried out at sites before contractors move in although they have their own projects too. Away from the major work, groups of local and visiting volunteers work on restoration and maintenance.

3 MG

The hours spent on restoration are recorded and can be used as matched funding against the major funding from the Heritage Lottery Fund.

Volunteers have two bases at Eastington and Eisey but can be found out and about wherever the work is to be done.

4 NB

at volunteers do

5 NB

There are towpath makers, towpath maintainers, lock and bridge rebuilders, dredger refurbishers and operators, engine maintainers, painters, tug and maintenance boat crew, a group preparing and selling logs and even volunteers who have been involved with the high-tech Hydro Project at Dudbridge.

Not all volunteers need to get their hands dirty. Some work to celebrate the canals by qualifying to provide boat trips for the public. Some work as volunteers, managing and staffing the two visitor centres promoting the work of the Trust. There's even a 'Roadshow' which takes the message out to venues both local and national. Some use their expertise as photographers or maintain the website and, last but not least, produce publications like the Trust's quarterly magazine or this book!

6 CT

Not all members need to be volunteers! Just being a member is a great help. Besides helping you keep in touch, every new member adds to the credibility of the project in the eyes of funders by showing the level of support for such a great project.

7 NB

1. Visitor Centre, Wallbridge, Stroud
2. Prince's Trust Volunteers Help Out
3. CCT Griffin's Mill Lock Volunteers
4. Waterways Recovery Group
5. Visitor Centre, Saul
6. Trip Boat *Perseverance* at Saul
7. Trip Boat *Endeavour* at Stonehouse
8. Trip Boat *Inglesham* at Lechlade

8 MG

Cotswolds Miscellany

As the end of this book is reached, it's time to mop up some of the things that have not received enough attention, so here's a summary. Take a look at the pictures opposite from the top.

The inscription can be found along the towpath near Bowbridge on a sturdy post.

Paddle gear for a lock is an essential mechanism which allows the lock to work. By attaching a windlass to the end of the long shaft on the left of the picture, it can be wound round. The cogs on the right hand side of the picture turn and raise the notched metal bar. This in turn is attached to a paddle (or door) covering a gap in the lock gate. This allows water in the lock to be let out.

The original design was deemed too dangerous to satisfy modern Health & Safety standards but there were conflicting interests that demanded that any new design should respect the canal's historic integrity. Enter Cotswold Canals Trust member, and retired engineer, Jim White who came up with the solution you see here. The paddle gear was machined within a mile of the canal.

Canal tokens were struck due to an insufficient supply of small coins in the 1700s. Common practice was followed when half penny tokens were struck for the Thames & Severn Canal to pay the workforce. They were accepted in local shops and pubs, being ultimately 'payable at Brimscombe Port'.

Milestones and mileplates were a feature of the Thames & Severn Canal. Walbridge is in Stroud and Inglesham is near Lechlade. The larger picture shows an original mileplate whilst the smaller one is a replica that can be found today alongside the towpath in Chalford.

More common alongside the towpath is a milestone without its plate like this one which is also in Chalford. They fell victim to souvenir hunters although today's location of a good number is known.

Father Thames was once found at the Source of the Thames but suffered from vandalism so was moved alongside St John's Lock, the highest on the Thames at Lechlade. He had started life in 1854 when he was created for an exhibition in Crystal Palace, London.

The Heritage Lottery Fund formally awarded £11.9 million in January 2006 towards the first phase of the restoration of the Cotswold Canals. This became known as Phase 1A (see the maps). At the same time the project was offered match funding of £6 million by the South West of England Regional Development Agency (SWRDA). Later, this government body was dissolved but the funding was safe.

Other contributors to the funding for the Phase 1A package include Stroud District Council (Lead Partner) and the Cotswold Canals Trust which committed to raise £800,000 as its financial contribution as well as over £1 million of volunteer effort.